the Diva Diaries
I0079569

"No one should have the power to define how you view yourself."

the Diva Diaries

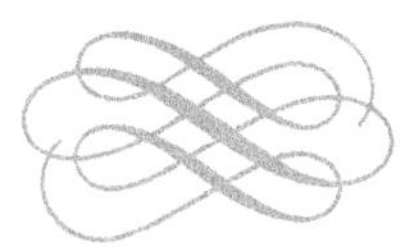

LIVING THROUGH TOUGH SEASONS

written & illustrated by

Crystal-Marie MITCHELL

The Diva Inc.
thedivainc.com
info@thedivainc.com

The Diva Diaries Living Through Tough Seasons

Cover & Interior Design: Crystal-Marie Mitchell
Cover Image & Author Picture: Jamison Boyer
Edited by: Meredith Clark
Published by: CreateSpace Independent Publishing Platform, North Charleston, SC

Printed in the United States of America

ISBN-10: 0692433546
ISBN-13: 978-0692433546

While the author has made every effort to provide accurate internet addresses for some content noted in the Notes section, the author nor the publisher is responsible for errors or changes made after publication.

ALL MY LOVE.

Wow! What a journey this has been. Let me first thank God for all of the lessons and for seeing me through times that I didn't think I was going to make it through. I give You praise for placing the desire to write this book in my heart. Without Your hand God, this book wouldn't be possible.

There are far too many people to name but I want to give a special shout out to my editor Dr. Meredith Clark for giving The Diva Diaries the push it needed to be better and finally make it to print.

Thank you to my parents for giving me life and love.

Thank you Lindsay and Felicia for reading the early drafts of the book and providing much needed feedback.

To my prayer warriors, I thank you for praying me through tough seasons.

Thank you Rachael for giving me the name Diva.

To Analena, Bronwyn, Kristine, Angela, Tanesha, Janice, and Rita, thank you for being angels on my journey in life and being a part of this story. Your presence in my life however long or short has been greatly appreciated and I hope each one of you knows how much I love you. I changed everyone else's names because it was more important to get the lesson but I included your names because I believe that what is done in secret should be rewarded openly. It is my way of thanking you - the angels that God has put in my life.

It is my sincere hope that each one of you that is reading this is blessed and finds a friend in these pages.

CONTENTS.

CONTENTS.

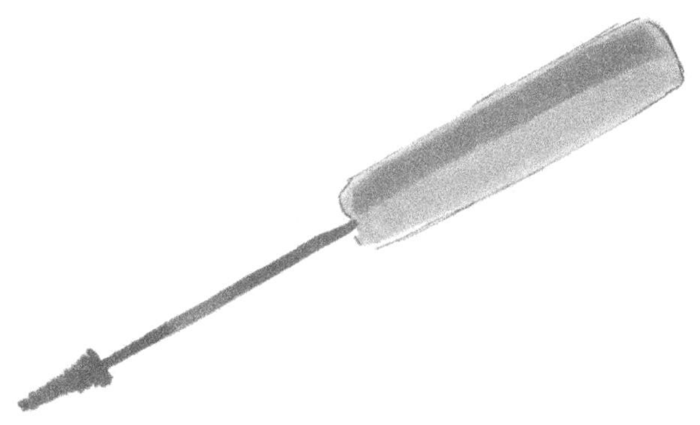

YOU ARE BEAUTIFUL!

BLESSED BEYOND MEASURE.

I'm holding on to the Lord's garment
Because that is the only thing I can do
You pushed me way past believing
Can't believe what you put me through
You had my faith all shook up
I lost my faith in true love

But I have a testimony
Used to give God glory
I'm a walking, living, breathing testimony
That's how the Lord gets His glory
Trials and tribulations just weren't for me
It was the Lord getting His glory

Broken but not destroyed
Blessed beyond measure
I'm still holding on
If it weren't for God
I don't know what I'd do
Can't believe I put any trust in you
Thank God for forgiveness
I am so blessed

BLESSED BEYOND MEASURE.

I can move on from your lies and into happiness

But I have a testimony
Used to give God Glory
I'm a walking, living, breathing testimony
That's how the Lord gets His glory
Trials and tribulations just weren't for me
It was the Lord getting His glory

I'm holding on to the Lord's garment
Because that is the only thing I can do
You pushed me way past believing
Can't believe what you put me through
You had my faith all shook up
I lost my faith in true love

But I have a testimony
Used to give God Glory

WHAT IS A DIVA?

I remember when my friend Rachael called me a diva for the first time. We were sitting on her couch a few days before Thanksgiving and she said:

"Crys Mitch (my college nickname), you are a DIVA."

I believe we were discussing if I could make it in a place like New York because I was in transition at the time. She was calling me a diva to give me encouragement that I could make it. That's when I fell in love with the term.

To me, a diva is someone who is very stylish. You may see her and make the mistake of believing that is all she is. But she is much more. She strives for excellence in all she does and aims to put her best foot forward in her work. She turns mistakes into opportunities to better educate herself. Obstacles become her stepping stones to greatness. She is fearfully and wonderfully made and turns heads when she walks — not necessarily because of what she is wearing, but because of the quiet and confident presence she exudes when she enters a room. She learns from her past and turns her lessons into a testimony to help others. She cries because life can be tough, but don't misunderstand her — she is not weak. She is a leader in most of what she does. Her friends look to her for inspiration and encouragement. But she is also willing to follow at times. She is fully capable of being independent, but would love to be interdependent with the right person. Her smile radiates and she is a walking testimony of God's grace and mercy.

Is she you?

1.
COMMENCEMENT.

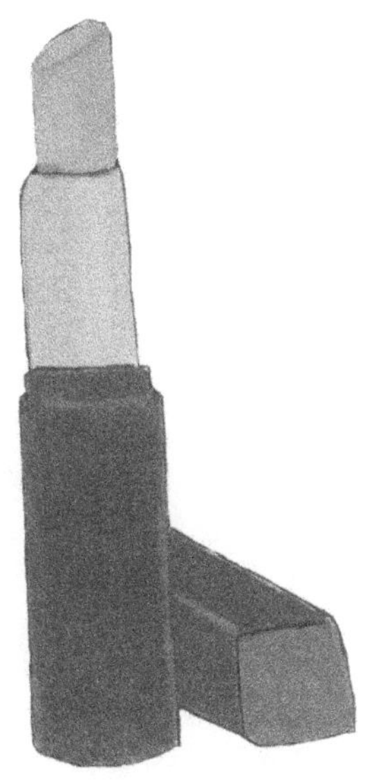

People tend to think a diva's life is always glamorous. I beg to differ. Life teaches everyone lessons in different ways, no matter how gorgeous you may be, or how much money you may or may not have. If you are a woman (or man) of faith, you know the Bible promises trouble during your time here on earth:

> "Man that is born of a women is of few days and full of trouble." ~Job 14:1 KJV

But do not fret; true divas are willing to help each other through these turbulent times by offering words of wisdom and encouragement. It is easy to feel alone. Believe me, for every one of your nights crying in the dark, there are hundreds of women who are shedding tears as well.

I've had my share of lonely, teary-eyed nights battling depression, navigating unhealthy relationships and surviving economic upset. But what I am figuring out is that these situations can't break you unless you let them. True divas have an inner determination that protects them and helps to project them into action when obstacles threaten their spirits. This inner determination comes from God. It's the way He shows you his purpose for your life.

I am currently living in San Francisco, my dream city. I earned my master's in Industrial Arts in 2009. With student loans to pay and a rough economy that forces me to stretch every dollar, living in San Francisco is costly. According to SFGate.com, of the 30 most common jobs in San Francisco, the salary ranges from $22,000 to $140,000[1].

One lesson life will teach you is that a true diva is resourceful. You are never alone, even when your circumstances appear otherwise. Once you become comfortable with yourself and your situation, it will be easier to reach out and ask for advice – or vent to the right people. I count myself lucky to have several women in my corner who are God's confirmation that my life has purpose. These women are sisters, friends, and family who have prayed me through tough times. They constantly remind me through speech and action that God is not through with me yet. If I had given up on life, I would not have written this book. There are people who will read this and be encouraged not to give up. That means that my life and my story has purpose. It's worth the fight. It's a life worth living.

Years ago, during my first year in graduate school, I stayed in the dorms. I had an undergraduate roommate who had her mother come up almost every weekend. One day her mother asked if anyone had been in our room. I said no and continued to watch TV in the living room. I do not allow people in my room when I share a room with other people. Then I could hear her mother start to say to my roommate and her father that the ink in the printer was missing. My roommate was white; I am African-American. Sitting in the living room listening, I knew where this was going to go. The next thing I know, I'm being accused of stealing printer ink. Printer ink? First of all, I am not a thief, and second, I didn't even have a printer. I was devastated. I know that racism exists. But I thought that moving to California would limit the amount of racism I would experience. It was then that I realized I was going to have to learn how to deal with problems that arose on my own — I was no longer in the relative safety of my parents' home.

I called my friend Tanesha. Then single, Tanesha was coming to a similar realization. She, too, was upset about her current living and financial situation. Our parents had been great providers and we found ourselves struggling to move beyond the girls we were and toward the life we always envisioned ourselves to have: the lives of truly independent women! We discussed the frustration we had with our bank accounts and the lack of money in them. We were working and going to school and for the first time paying bills ourself.

It's crazy to think back on that conversation. I can now say that I had plenty of money back then. I was not used to having to pay all of my bills myself. I mean, I had a daddy which was at times my personal ATM. I joke, but in all seriousness, my qualms about not having enough money at that time was nothing compared to the seasons I would go through much later in life after that call.

While the content of this book commenced well before then, it was because of that call with Tanesha and my discussion with Rachael that I decided to call this book, The Diva Diaries. I am letting you into my life as I find my inner DIVA, so that you can be comforted on your journey. Walking into your purpose can be difficult. I've had my share of rejections that lead me through a young life of depression and self-esteem issues. Life can have you feeling rejected and oppressed. Seasons can come and go and you will still feel like you are stagnant. Be comforted, my sister, and continue to walk.

This book tackles a plethora of issues relating to the young and determined diva: feeling alone, wondering where God is, how to choose healthy relationships, living posh on any budget, what it truly means to be wealthy, and so much more. It is my goal that this book will be one of the inspirational tools you turn to when you are in need of solid advice, comfort or a good laugh. Most of all, it is my sincere desire that you will find companionship and a partner to grow with in these pages. I will grow with you.

Be comforted, my sister, and continue to persevere.

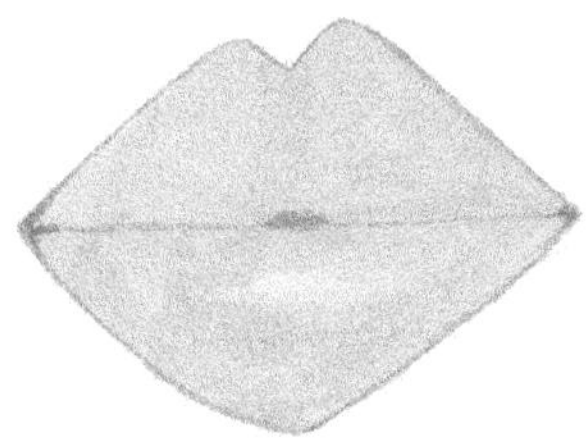

2.
LESSONS ON THE LUNCH YARD.

In 1993, my family broke the news to me that I would be leaving Belton, Missouri, for San Francisco. Belton had been my home since I was two or three years old. We lived on Richards-Gebaur Air Force Base. Yes, I was a military brat... and proud! Most of what I remember about the little town of Belton and my life there was pleasant. I remember being well-known. Being the only black kid in your elementary school will do that for you. My mother always had a theme for my birthday parties and they were well attended. I was invited to spend the night parties on my friends' farms and hayrides with others. I guess you could say I was a country girl. It's funny to think about it now. I consider myself to be a major city girl.

One of the most disappointing memories I can remember is when I gave a guy I liked in the third or fourth grade a ring my uncle had given me, and the boy gave it to another girl. Talk about cold-blooded. That must have been my first broken heart. I was crushed. But that heartbreak paled in comparison to hearing the news that I would be leaving the only home I knew for California.

When I look back on it, this wasn't my worst memory of Missouri. I was walking down my street on the military base I lived on when a black dog came up to me and started barking viciously. I thought he was going to attack me, so I screamed. The owner, a white woman with short black hair came out and said that the dog didn't like black people. I didn't get it then. I guess I was too young to understand how a dog doesn't like black people. I get it now, and it has nothing to do with the dog. But even with these few poor memories, Missouri was my home.

My grandmother always recounts when she told me that I would be a California girl. My reply to her?, *"I don't want to be a California girl!"* When I look back into my memory of the long drive from Missouri to California, I can hear myself repeating that line in my head while laying stretched across the backseat of my parents' 1989 Camaro. I am sure my parents had a great deal of important worries about moving, but my only concerns were making new friends, getting adjusted to a new school, and getting good grades.

STARTING OVER

When we arrived in San Francisco we prepared to move into our new home just seconds away from the Golden Gate Bridge. So many boxes to unpack. I couldn't wait to get settled and meet new friends.

I started the fifth grade at Cabrillo Elementary School. This was a whole new world for me and I was very open and curious about its differences. It was the first time I was introduced to new cultures. Although I lived on a military base, I rarely remember seeing other races other than African American and Caucasian. There were a few Samoans that I knew while living in Missouri.

My favorite thing to do was collect stickers (Hello Kitty, anyone?) and play this game where you have to jump over a rope made of rubber bands with a few of my Asian classmates. I was fascinated with Asian culture, and I still am.

NOBODY LIKES ME

According to my fifth-grade diary (which I am reading now as I write this) most of the entries are about school and boys. No surprise there. But the entry I made in mauve marker, two days after my 11th birthday on April 28, 1994, foreshadowed the next year to come.

> "My birthday party is tomorrow. I can't wait...
> I'm going to middle school. Sixth grade.
> Nobody likes me."

Nobody likes me? Although I did not elaborate on why I thought so in that entry, I do remember feeling rejected by everyone around me. It is a feeling that began around that day and lasted for years to come.

The diary entries from my fifth-grade year are filled with words by a young girl trying to find herself. I can look back now and see that I was so desperately wanting to be accepted and desired. I can't fathom why this was so important for me. Why was this my focus? If I knew then what I know now, I would have loved myself and would not be concerned with the opinions of the boys I was trying to attract and the girls who were also suffering with low self-esteem.

It is evident in the pages of my young diary that my younger self needed some self-esteem...bad. Each page was filled with a new love interest. What was I searching for? Entries about Kamirian (whom you will meet later in the book) were plentiful. In fact, he was the last entry in one of my diaries. His rejection would send me down a path of depression and self-hatred.

It is fascinating to look back at my young self through words on a page. While I've learned to accept that people may not like you for one reason or another, as a preteen, my whole world was wrapped in people's perception of me.

Even in this diary entry, I was excited for middle school. It was going to be something new – the beginning of growing up! All of the middle school kids rode the public bus in San Francisco and I was going to be one of those kids – practically an adult.

My first day in middle school I got lunch with Angela and sat outside (I do not remember us eating in a formal cafeteria). Angela was a skinny Korean girl with long black hair and large cheeks. She and I lived in a duplex on the Presidio, and like me she was a military brat and an only child. I laid my purse down on the bench and sat down to eat. I cannot remember what I had for lunch, but when I got up to throw away my trash, a swarm of kids huddled over the bench. When I returned, the contents of my purse had been emptied out; my sanitary napkins were strewn on the ground (I carried these although I had not yet started my period) and my lunch money for the week had been stolen. My first day in middle school brought my first lesson in reality: Never leave your purse unattended, even if the trash can is only two feet away. The deeper lesson: not everyone is trustworthy. Given the opportunity, some will become thieves.

"The Deeper Lesson: not everyone is trustworthy..."

Fortunately, I was privileged to get the money I needed for lunch again from my parents. I am old enough now to understand that the kids who stole from me may not have had access to the same kind of resources. Though I do not excuse thievery, those kids' families may not have had the means to give them money, so they resorted to stealing. Or maybe they were just cruel. In either case, I feel bad for them and thankful to them. Becoming a thief at a young age can only lead you down the wrong path. I can only imagine what they are up to now. But their petty theft taught me to be more aware of my surroundings — and the people who are around me.

From the first day of sixth grade, God was preparing me for the life He wanted me to have and the lessons He wanted me to learn. The next lesson I would learn would come to me in the seventh grade: *rejection.*

DIVA RECAP:

- Not everyone who is around you has your best interest at heart, and given the opportunity, they can hurt you. This doesn't mean you shouldn't trust people. Just be cautious and aware of your surroundings.
- God uses experiences large and small to teach you lessons throughout life. Learn the lesson the first time so you can move on.

3.

REJECTION.

> "No one should have the power to define how you view yourself."

I attended Marina Middle School for both sixth and seventh grade. Middle school in San Francisco was a far cry from elementary school and an even farther cry from my Missouri hayrides. I was introduced to gangs and people with different socioeconomic statuses than me. It is something I can see clearly now but as a young preteen I could not.

Marina was a large light grey two story building in the shape of a "U". The building was gated and the lunch yard sat in the middle of the "U". You could hear the roar of kids playing on the yard and in my case, the whisper of kids teasing me.

In middle school, the kids were extremely cruel to me. The teasing surpassed normal (if teasing is normal) and left me going home in fear many days. The "mean girls" would threaten to beat me up because they did not like my shoes. I realize now that they saw the Diva in me even before I did. My preternatural seventh-grade style was my mom's doing. My shoes were Nine West when everyone else was wearing Nike. My hair was down and curled when they were wearing braids. They were attacking me for being different. But at age 11, you do not realize that your peers are insecure themselves. All you know is that they don't like you. And during those preteen years, being liked was all that mattered.

> "To all of my haters…I appreciate you because you hated me on a level that I didn't even know I was on."
> -Bishop T.D. Jakes[2]

I remember sitting in Mr. Tse's math class when a "friend" Donna, came up to hug me. She rubbed her hand on my back and asked me how I was doing. Donna was a biracial girl with long, shiny, curly, black hair. I thought nothing of the exchange, and sat down to work on math problems. I got up, presumably to sharpen my pencil, when I felt a jolt in my back. Eric, my Samoan friend with a long ponytail and gorgeous tan (whom I had known in Missouri), kicked me in my back. When I asked him why he kicked me, he replied, *"Because the sign on your back said so."*

Yes, that "friendly" rub on the back from Donna turned out to be her opportunity to paste a cruel sign on my back. How hurtful this was. I felt defeated. These two didn't just put a sign on my back, they bruised my spirit. Was this funny? I was that girl. The one I thought only existed in cheesy teen dramas. The girl who got "kick me" signs taped to her back because other kids thought it was funny. How did I become this girl? Why did I become this girl? Tormented during recess and after school by the children in the schoolyard, and left alone by my "friends," I was often left with nowhere to turn for comfort.

What I wish I could have understood then is that not everyone who calls themselves a friend truly is one. Friendships require commitment and trust. How can you stand beside someone you call a friend and see them getting verbally or physically abused? Worse, how can you be a part of the abuse?

MY SHOES

I was always getting threats of getting beat up — and for what? One day while I was at lunch with my good friend Analena (whom I now consider an angel), a tall, skinny brown-skinned black girl came up to us. She addressed Annie, Analena's nickname, in a positive way, and then proceeded to tell me that she didn't like my shoes. Most of the time I got teased, I would say nothing and just cry about it when I got home. This time I decided to stick up for myself I told the girl that she didn't have to like my shoes. After all they weren't hers, right? Her response? *"I'm going to beat you up after school."* I was terrified. It was like waiting all day for a spanking from your parents. Every time I saw her in the hallway, she would give me a look. When Annie and I were getting dressed for gym class she came around to remind me of the butt kicking she was going to deliver that afternoon. Annie told her that she needed to leave me alone. Annie was Austrian and Nigerian and had black, shiny, tight curly hair. She always seemed confident and comfortable in her skin. Just her sticking up for me gave me a sigh of relief. And that butt kicking? It never came. I have Annie to thank for that. But that experience made it hard for me to stand up for myself.

When things like this happened and I was at home, once my homework was done and my family had retired for the evening, I meditated on the fear and harassment, silently crying myself to sleep. I started calling myself all the names I was called. I started believing what the bullies were saying and gave them power over me that was never theirs to have.

THE SAMANTHA CLUB

One day I was walking home from the bus stop with Angela and a friend from church when that friend asked me if she should invite Samantha to her birthday party. I was baffled. We all went to the same school, and there was no one named Samantha. Angela was quiet. Getting the sense that something was amiss, I said:

"If Samantha is your friend you should invite her. If not, you shouldn't."

I cannot remember if I found out in that moment or the next day or so. But my so-called friends had made up something called The Samantha Club so they could talk about me in front of my face. One of the guys in my shop class explained to me who "Samantha" was. Yes, even the guys knew that these cruel young girls wanted to talk about me to my face and use a code name for it. Now that I am writing this out, I can feel the hurt and anger come rushing back. Wooo-saaa!

I did get invited to the birthday party. There was no way this friend was not going to be able to invite me because our families were so close. While at the all-girls' birthday party, the attendees decided that they should have an intervention and tell me that I should change my attitude. Wait?!! What??!! My attitude? The only one who stood up for me was Analena. I remember her saying something like,

"There is no need for you to change who you are and keep doing you."

I was hurt and I wanted to go home. Also something I could not do because then my "friend" would get in trouble

— her parents would be alerted to what was going on in the basement. How hurtful! I learned another lesson during that time: people will be cruel to you, and then make it seem as though their shortcomings are your fault. Nothing I did could have warranted such poor treatment; anything I did do would have been in my own self-defense. Words and actions do hurt. This hurt me to the core. It was only compounded by Kamirian's rejection.

A BROKEN HEART LEADS TO BROKEN RELATIONSHIPS

I met Kamirian in the seventh grade. He was beautiful – caramel skin with lusciously large brown eyes and black curly hair. Think of a young version of Christian Keyes or a taller Tahj Mowry. Standing next to him and looking at his smile was like a Crest bright white commercial. *Queue the bright white smile 'ding!' sound here.

Carl Pickhardt, Ph.D, says that teens usually start significant dating between the ages 15-18 during their high school years[3]. My parents did not allow me to date until I was 16. But that did not stop me from having crushes nor did it actually stop me from having a "boyfriend." I simply had to be secretive if I liked someone or when my feelings got hurt because a boy didn't like me. Technically, I wasn't supposed to have been interested anyway. I couldn't help how I felt and my parents were not going to understand nor tolerate the fact that I liked boys way before I turned 16. So I had to keep the way I felt about Kamirian a secret. I was only 11 or 12. Sixteen was years away, but you couldn't tell my heart that. It was more than a crush to me.

He was my first love — if you could call it that. Even then I was destined to be a designer - I loved beautiful things. And Kamirian was just that. He was the most attractive boy I had ever met. I couldn't wait for gym class each day. We all had to line up and sit according to our gym numbers and Kamirian sat in front of me at a diagonal. I wanted so badly to run my fingers through his hair. Every once in a while he would turn back and smile. He wasn't smiling at me, he was smiling at the girl sitting next to me. But I still appreciated the smile. It sounds silly as an adult, but the 11-year-old me thought if he would be my boyfriend maybe everyone else would like me.

I remember asking a friend of mine to tell him that I liked him. She said she tried and told him that we would be cute together because our real names were similar. But according to Kamirian, I was not his type. I will never know how you get a "type" at age 11. But it was this rejection coupled with the bullying from the previous year that shaped my self esteem and the way I chose to date for years following. I gave the power over my self-esteem to my peers at an early age. I listened to their cruel teasing and subconsciously handed them power over my self worth. The key to self worth and self-esteem is that it can only come from self. No one should have the power to define how you view yourself.

In preteen language, saying someone is not your type is the equivalent of saying you are not cute enough or at all. I was not pretty enough. I was not good enough. My complexion was not fair enough. I was not curvy enough. I was just not enough! And I began to say this to myself daily. That year, he dated two of my friends – including Annie – and sadly, this made me feel worse. I was not good enough, but they were?

Then, at the end of my seventh-grade year, my father decided to move the family across the country to Orange Park, Florida, so that he could plan for retiring and purchasing a home. But that was 3,000 miles away from Kamirian. The distance did not stop me from pursuing him. If I could get him to like me, it would prove to all my middle school bullies and myself that I was good enough, pretty enough. For 10 years, I wrote him letters and poems and sent pictures every week – sometimes 4-page letters (as if I wrote that song for Aaliyah). I sent each one of these letters in hopes that one day he would write back. I was young and insecure and writing Kamirian was my way of showing my "love."

When I was a junior in high school, after I called Kamirian and he let his friends be quite rude to me, I decided I had enough. All those years of writing him and I had not received one letter back from him. In my last letter to Kamirian, I told him that I had been in California and did not come see him because I didn't think he wanted me to. This was true. I had just made it back to Florida from an FBLA (Future Business Leaders of America) National Competition in Los Angeles. Sure, I wasn't exactly in San Francisco, but I remember making that letter sound like I was. Would you believe that shortly after that I received my first and only letter from Kamirian?

The letter, dated 9.19.00, was written in pencil. I remember going to the mailbox and seeing this letter. I rushed inside, went to my room, shut the door and began reading it over and over. Not only had he written me a letter, he'd sent pictures too, which had my young heart racing.

Hey, What's up?

Yeah, Surprise - Surprise! I am finally sending you a letter. But let's not dwell on that simple fact.

First let me apologize for not responding. I guess it its hard for me to see why you would put [in] the effort when I was so immature in the "seventh grade".

I feel terrible and I hope you forgive me and realize, I have MATURED!!!

So don't get the feeling that I don't want to see you because I do. (Thanks for all the pictures). I hope we can write back and forth now that I have written back.

Anyways, how are you? Me-I'm cool, taking care of school, cause last year I really messed up. How about you? Is it hot, because it's scorching out here. Well I would write more but I have to do some homework.

P.S. I sent you some pictures (finally), I hope you like them.

~Kamirian

This letter was everything to me. After reading this I thought, "Wow, he appreciated all of my effort," and he asked for forgiveness. Did receiving this letter make my feelings and self-esteem journey better or worse?

The truth is the damage had been done. I spent years telling myself I wasn't good enough and that destroyed my self-esteem. Be careful what seeds you sow and what ground you sow them on. ***Matt. 13:3-9***

SUICIDAL THOUGHTS

Thank God for angels. I remember having a moment where I wanted to end it all. It was a very real moment for me. All I remember is waking up the next morning. I know that I was crying and it was a lonely and dangerous moment of thoughts for me. But I cannot tell you what happened between thinking about killing myself and waking up that next morning okay. All I can say is that God had a better plan. [According to the CDC (Center for Disease Control and Prevention) suicide is the third leading cause of death for youth ages 10-24[4].

Suicide and suicidal thoughts are permanent solutions to a temporary problem. If you are having these thoughts, I would definitely seek out some one you trust or contact one of the national suicide hotlines. Suicide Prevention Lifeline 1.800.273.8255 suicidepreventionlifeline.org[5]]

During those 10 years, I aggressively pursued guys who

reminded me of Kamirian. But it never proved to work out. They had to look like him or remind me of him in someway, mostly in physical appearance.

In high school, my depressive state could no longer hide itself in between my tear-soaked pillows at night. One weekend, I was sitting with my girlfriends Janice and Tanesha. As we were discussing our senior year in high school, I began to cry. The carefully concealed hurt that stemmed from middle school had finally caught up with me and I could not handle it on my own anymore. I turned to them and said, "Guys, I think I need help." My friends both looked at each other and then at me, and Tanesha replied, in the most sincere voice, "I think so, too."

I called my mother immediately and told her and she set me up with a therapist. After three sessions, I no longer saw the point of going. At the time, I thought I knew the problem, I just could not control the solution. I thought the problem was that Kamirian did not see me as beautiful; the solution was to dye my hair and wear hazel contact lenses and do whatever it took to make my self feel more beautiful. But the true problem was that I did not see myself as beautiful.

DIVA RECAP:

- No one has the power to control your self-esteem if you don't give it to them.
- You have every right to stand up for yourself and people who do not want you to will often try to oppress your desire to speak up.
- The seeds you plant will grow into fruit. Sow wisely.
- It's okay to ask for help.
- Choose to live. Always.

4.
SELF-ESTEEM.

If women were created beautiful and man was made in God's own image, then why are we still struggling to see our individual beauty? ***Genesis 1:27***

We become chameleons, changing with every relationship we enter. One guy says we are too big and we spend hours in the gym — all to have our next boyfriend tell us he likes his women large. When did we begin letting men and/or society define how we think of ourselves?

It sounds ridiculous to think that most women change their appearance and other parts of their personality to attract a certain type of man or to fit into a group when they are meant to stand out. Perhaps you are saying to yourself that this isn't you. But no one is watching while you read this, nor can they hear your private thoughts. So go ahead and be honest with yourself.

Think to a time in your life, young or old, when you changed something about yourself based on the media, a boyfriend, or a friend's comment. I'll wait. I'm sure if you are honest with yourself, this has happened more times then you would like to count.

In high school a friend of mine suggested that I walk down the hall without my glasses. I can barely see my hand without my glasses, but I took her suggestion and muddled my way through the crowded halls of my high school. Heads turned and people began telling me how good I looked without my glasses. It was that day that I went home and began to pressure my mother and father for contact lenses. Soon, I was donning my signature hazel contacts. I only wore my glasses at night and people never saw me in them. As a matter of fact, I only began to become comfortable wearing my glasses out in public when I was in graduate school.

I don't know if this moment has come for you or when it will, but I realized that I cannot spend my life trying to live up to someone else's expectation. One thing is for sure, every love interest, ex-boyfriend, and frienemy I've had taught me about myself–what I will live with and what I will not.

There were countless nights that I spent telling myself that I was not beautiful; I projected that broken image of myself. It's amazing how when you're feeling bad about yourself, you will attract people who are not going to treat you well. It's the law of attraction — you attract what you put out. I wish I had known this when I was growing up, it would've saved me countless heartbreaks. People will only treat you how you let them — and how you let them treat you is based on how you see yourself. Do yourself a favor and see yourself how God sees you.

God loves you and wants to use you just the way you are. All of the trials that you are going through will become your testimony and catapult you into your destiny. Why ruin this blessing by thinking of yourself as less than God does. Why let someone that didn't create you define how you feel about yourself.

The thing about self-esteem is that it has to be self that drives it. No man, friend, amount of money, social status, or magazine should control how you feel about yourself. I, along with many of my friends, have struggled with low self-esteem. I've had to work hard to build confidence in myself and my abilities. When people see me, I'm sure that they've always thought that I've been a confident person. Like a lot of women with insecurities and low self-esteem, I managed to hide my feelings of inadequacy behind my smile and my sense of humor.

Getting in touch with your self-esteem and building confidence is always going to be a struggle. As the seasons of your life change, so might your feelings about your self and your self-worth. But if you practice developing a healthy confidence in your talents, and surround yourself with people who can affirm you and pray you through tough seasons, it makes the journey a lot more bearable.

These are some of the tips that I put into practice in my life to build a healthy self-esteem and to affirm myself and those around me:

#1: POSITIVE MEDITATION/AFFIRMATIONS.

Find a favorite quote or Bible verse and repeat it to yourself when you think that you are getting down. If you're struggling with believing that you were physically beautiful, look in the mirror and tell yourself you are beautiful each day. It may feel weird at first, but it is the beginning to seeing your true self. There are always things that women wish they could change about their physical appearance. But remember, while it's admirable to strive toward perfection, beauty is much more than physical. Affirming yourself with daily quotes or positive meditation will make you feel beautiful and you will project this beauty outward.

One of my favorite Bible verses that I learned when I had to memorize it for Bible study is Philippians 4:6.

"Be careful for nothing; but in everything by prayer and supplication with thanksgiving let your requests be made known to God."

#2: PAMPER YOURSELF!

Make sure to take the proper time for yourself. Whether it's taking that quiet moment and reflecting or treating yourself to a mani/pedi, you must make the time for you. It does not matter what is going wrong or right in your life, pampering is a necessity.

#3: ACCEPT YOU!

Yes, you have flaws. Guess what? You are still a Diva! Acknowledge your weaknesses and work on minimizing and eliminating them. But do not beat yourself up. Doing so is counterproductive and accomplishes nothing. Accentuate your best features (personality included) and work on your negative ones.

#4: PRAYING SISTERS

Sometimes you can't do it alone, and that's when God sends other women to surround you with love and prayer. I've been lucky to have God-fearing women in my life who have prayed for me during times when I could not pray for myself. They have kept me and guided me and made sure that whatever happened in my life I didn't give up. If you don't have these type women in your life I would recommend that you find a good church, talk to some of the mothers of the church, or find some women to connect with on this level.

There are very few women that I will allow to pray with or over me. With these women I've developed a very honest and open relationship with no judgements. The relationship that I have with them is a two-way street and it takes time to build that trust.

#5: LET GO!

There are some things that you will never be able to control. Stop trying. Let it go. This goes for friendships as well as romantic relationships. Sometimes friendships dissolve because life has you going in different directions. Cherish the friends that you're meant to keep and understand that not everybody will remain in your inner circle. Some men will never love you properly even if you stay and try to be the best woman that you could be. It doesn't matter what was said in the past – if God is trying to tear something away from you stop trying so fervently to hold onto it. Let it go.

Trust me, I've had to repeat this to myself several times in the last few years. It's not easy. Sometimes we internalize what went wrong in a relationship and the truth is it had nothing to do with us. Pray about it and once you do move on.

DIVA RECAP:

- The changes you make in life should be about your personal growth and development and not for anyone else.
- You will attract what you put out. Be confident and love yourself.
- Let go of the things God is trying to pull from you.

5.

WAIT FOR YOU.

I was on the telephone with my guy friend after sending him an email about how depressing my dating life was and how confused I was as to why I was still single. I must have scared him a little because as soon as he received it he gave me a call.

"What is wrong with me?" I asked him. I guess you can consider that a loaded question, but after a few hours of conversation he made me realize two important things that I am compelled to pass on to you: One, you are perfect for the person who is perfect for you. Two, while dating, even the relationships that don't work are not a waste of time.

"You are perfect for the person who is perfect for you."

Dating can be a tricky situation. Most people start dating in their teenage years, long before they can clearly identify who they are. While you have to start somewhere, dating while still trying to figure out yourself is often difficult.

When I was in the seventh grade, I met Kamirian, who was so attractive to me with his large black curly hair, gorgeous big brown eyes, and mocha complexion that his rejection sent me off the deep end. (See Chapter 3: Rejection) I did not know who I was or what I was worth at that age. I let an early rejection dictate my life for years to come. After this rejection, most of my boyfriends/love interests had similar characteristics to Kamirian.

For years following, I would lay awake at night crying and beating myself up for not being beautiful enough, smart enough, or just enough. I didn't know it but even then God had a purpose for all of this. Many boyfriends and breakdowns later, I realized that I had given power over my self worth to someone that God never meant to have it.

All through my early dating life and college dating life

I was somewhat of a chameleon. One boyfriend would not like something about me and I would change it, another this and another that. I lost myself trying to be wanted – mistaking attention for love. Most of these boys did not know themselves enough to know what they truly wanted from a woman.

I've often contemplated why some of my relationships have been strained. I often blamed the other person in the process. And while they may have added to the issues in the relationship, they are not solely to blame. Whether I want to admit it or not, many of the problems in my relationships have been because of me. Somewhere on this road of life, I neglected to learn how to set proper BOUNDARIES.

Ahhh...boundaries.

I am finally learning the lesson I wish I knew years ago. In most of my relationships (especially ones with a significant other), I am a giver. I try to anticipate someone's need and supply it. I try to point out areas where they can grow. I put them before me. When they are sick I rush to be by their side. I look for ways to keep them happy.

Then if the relationship ends sourly I wonder, "Why?" It is because those necessary boundaries were not set.

"Do not make someone your priority
while you are just their option."

You have to take care of yourself in all relationships. Take time to evaluate if there is mutual giving. No one is in a relationship for it to be one-sided. Are you truly happy or are you trying to create a facade of happiness? Look and see if your actions are being reciprocated. Does this person fill you up as much as they take from you?

Women especially are naturally wired — and extensively groomed — to be nurturing. And with a nurturing spirit comes giving. But sometimes we tend to over do it. Take a step back and reevaluate your boundaries. If there are none present in your current relationships, be it work, personal or family related, set some. What do you want to get out of this relationship? What do you want to give? How will you evaluate if you should continue to foster the growth in this relationship?

When I was younger I used to ignore the flags that would come up in my relationships. I would say to myself, "Oh it will go away." How foolish of me. Those flags sprouted for a reason. No one can be in a bad relationship if they make the choice not to subject themselves to one. Those yellow flags that went off on the first date are just warning signs for the red ones you will see later in the relationship.

BARBEQUE BLUES

I can't remember how we actually met. I believe we had

mutual friends and we went to different high schools. He was two years older than me and we began casually dating (dating with no boyfriend/girlfriend title). I wanted a title like girlfriend and he wasn't interested in giving me that title. Something I didn't realize until much later.

He was a bit taller than me (I was 5'5"), had milk chocolate brown skin, and a slim build. Let's call him Jordan (names have been changed to protect the guilty...ha!). He met my mom and dad several times and was often at our family barbecues. My mom loved him, my dad not so much.

One day he called me up to ask me to go to a barbecue at his friends house. The caveat? I had to drive to the party where he already was. I figured that's not a problem, I have a car. In an excited frenzy, I ran in to ask my parents and my dad went ballistic. *"If he cannot pick you up then you cannot go!"* But what was the big deal? I had a car and it wasn't the 1950s–women do drive on dates. Ha! How naïve.

What I didn't understand until recently was that my father wanted me to know my worth. If this guy wanted me to go to the barbecue, then he should have been man enough to come to my father's door and ask him if I could go.

Alas, I went to the barbecue, and three years later ended up crying on the floor over a broken heart. If I would not have ignored that red flag at age 16, I could have saved myself a shattered heart and many pints of cookies 'n' cream ice cream.

Young divas reading this (and older ones who have yet to learn this lesson) take note: You deserve to be treated like a princess. Do you know what a princess is? She is a future Queen. If "Prince Charming" cannot get out of his carriage and knock on your door, then he's probably just masquerading. And that makes for a bad fairy tale. Let him go and move on.

No one will take care of you better than you.

"Keep thy heart with all diligence; for out of it are the issues of life."

~Proverbs 4:23

DIVA RECAP:

- Take the time to evaluate all of your relationships.
- Set boundaries.
- There is someone out there that is perfect for you. Wait for them.
- Pay attention to all flags in a relationship. They are there to tell you something.
- You are worth it. Don't let anyone treat you as if you are not.

6.

SENSATIONALLY SINGLE.

I can't say for sure if it is cultural or just something in my gut, but I have always wanted to be married. I've never been the type of woman who dated more than one guy at a time – I was always in it to win it. But here I am, single, never married and err...loving it!

Sure, every now and then I walk past those bridal magazines and wish I could pick them up for myself. But I was very content when I thumbed through them to give ideas to my BFF for her wedding in 2010.

It wasn't easy for me to get to the point where I am completely happy with being single. I had to go through an exhausting relationship where I was the giver and the other person the taker to realize that I would rather be single than be in an emotionally draining relationship.

I had been single for about four years and was loving it when I started writing this chapter. I was finding out new things about myself and what I was capable of doing. During this time in my life it wasn't easy financially because I had been laid off two jobs in a short period of time. I then found a great and steady job and my focus was less on finding a significant other (though at times I was lonely) and more about making myself the best single me I could be.

I remember finally getting to a consistently happy place by using the steps I've mentioned and shifting my focus. Many people told me the cliché saying, "Mr. Right comes when you are not looking." Well so does Mr. I Just Want To Mess Up Your Happy!

An old acquaintance called me on my birthday. I will have to save the full story for my next book but let's just say not every old saying applies. The relationship started wonderfully and it was starting to look like the cherry on top of my already-happy sundae. But this relationship almost destroyed all of the work I had put into being happy. It's as if the devil knew that since I was shifting my focus to God, self and living, he wanted to destroy my life. The sad thing? I almost let him.

So I cannot let this chapter pass without giving you tips to protect your happy.

#1: PROTECT YOUR HEART.

What looks good isn't always good for you. Sure it's cliché and we've all heard it before. But if we take this to heart and start analyzing the people and things we let into our lives we would be better off for it. This is true in all types of relationships not just romantic ones.

In high school, I had a guy friend that I had known since middle school. I'm sure that there were rumors that we dated but we did not. We would take turns treating each other to lunch, dinner or whatever we were doing to hang out. He was a very funny guy that I was not at all attracted to so it made for a good friendship. At least for me.

Our last year of high school I finally got the nerve to ask a mutual friend of ours to the prom. Yes, I was the one who asked, but we will address that later. My guy friend – whom we will call Jerry – knew how much I liked this other guy. I had a crush on him all four years of high school. Sarah, a good girlfriend at the time, told me that I should go ask him to the prom. With her vote of confidence in me, I asked. I walked up to his hotel room (we were at another FBLA conference) swallowed my pride and nervousness and said: *"Hi, Terrance, it's our senior year and I would love it if you would be my date to the prom."* His face replied way before his mouth did. His expression went from light and chipper to disgusted. He then said, *"Oh, why did you ask me that?"*

And then he shut the door. I was heartbroken. You can imagine what this did for my already shaky self-esteem.

You may be wondering what this has to do with Jerry. After a few days of crying and trying to mend my broken spirit

I went to the mall with Jerry and another mutual friend of ours to shop for prom attire. Jerry then tells me that Sarah, the same girlfriend who told me to ask Terrance to the prom would be going to the prom with him. I immediately went to defend her. *"She wouldn't do that to me. She is a true friend and I will call her right now to prove it to you."* As I am writing this, I can still hear the passion in my voice and feel the trust I had in her. I can also see the sly smirk on Jerry's face as I called her. She responded in this soft and genuinely sorry voice, *"I was going to talk to you about it."* My heart sunk into my stomach and I hung up the phone. Jerry looked at me as to say, "checkmate." I felt defeated and betrayed by two friends.

I later found out Jerry had orchestrated the two of them getting together. Knowing how I felt about Terrance and how I adored my good friend Sarah at the time, Jerry set me up to watch me get hurt.

Sarah and I had the same first period class and when it came time to sign yearbooks, I turned around to ask her to sign mine. I was hurt, believe me. But she was still a friend whom I loved and ultimately wished the best for. But I cut ties with Jerry. That is when I understood more that not all people that call themselves friends truly are.

Now over a decade later, Terrance and Sarah are married and have a beautiful family. I am so happy for them. I love seeing pictures of their kids on Facebook, it gives me nothing but great joy. I've learned that God is a God of order. What He wants to put together He will. Sometimes he will use circumstances that will teach you a hard lesson, yet those same circumstances that are tough for you will be a blessing for other people involved. My lesson was their blessing.

#2: EVALUATE YOUR RELATIONSHIPS.

Even in friendships, there is a reason why we are in a

relationship with that person. They make us laugh, are great shopping buddies, prayer partners or coworkers who turned into friends. Whatever the reason for entering into a relationship, make sure to evaluate the relationship regularly. What is it you want to get from this relationship? What do you want to give? Is this person draining or filling you? Are you in this relationship out of guilt, obligation, or comfort?

A great book that will help you dive deeper into relationships is Van Moody's "The People Factor: How building Great Relationships and Ending Bad Ones Unlocks Your God Given Purpose[6]." He provides exercises at the end of each chapter that will help you evaluate the relationships you are in and what type of friend YOU are.

#3: SET YOUR INTENT

I was at Oprah's Live the Life You Want Tour in San Jose,

California when she made it clear that you are responsible for your intentions. Its something that stuck with me. Now in my relationships, work and organizations that I volunteer with, I always ask myself what is my intent. In other words, why am I doing A, B, C, etc. When you start to understand your own intentions it is easier to let some things go and not be so overwhelmed. Sometimes we stay in relationships or volunteer with certain organizations out of obligation. And this is no way to operate.

#4: BE GRACEFUL!

Do not just walk and speak gracefully, but also give grace to others. God has forgiven you and allowed his grace to cover you–remember this the next time someone offends you. It will be a great time to pass them a generous helping of grace.

#5: FORGIVE YOURSELF

Forgiveness can be a constant battle. I mean who wants to forgive a person that hurt you to the core. For me, after I have processed and prayed over a situation I find it easy to forgive others. Truly easy. But forgiving myself is another story. Even after praying and asking forgiveness from God, I struggle with forgiving myself. And who am I to do so when God Himself has forgiven me. I am hardest on myself. But you really have to get to a point where you LET IT GO! You cannot change the mistakes you made but you can learn from them. To protect your happy you have to forgive yourself for the mistakes you made and ask others to do the same.

8 RELAXING WAYS TO BE IN YOUR OWN PRESENCE

I realized that it is also okay to pamper yourself. Not just the physical pampering but mentally too. Sometimes as women we carry loads that seem heavier than our capability. So it is necessary for us to understand the situation we live in and accept that sometimes we need to take care of ourselves before we break. This doesn't mean that you are weak. On the contrary, it means that you are among the many women who have learned that you cannot take care of anyone if you have not taken proper care of yourself first.

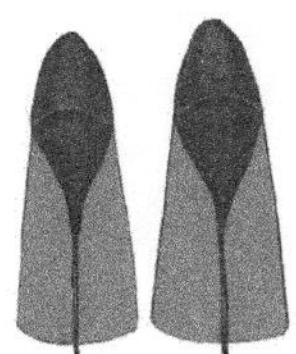

#1: TREAT YOURSELF!

I cannot stress this enough. Find a way to treat yourself. Make sure to regularly do something for you. Even if that means staying home and doing nothing.

#2: TURN YOUR PHONE OFF!

We spend entirely too much time on our techy gadgets. I've been turning my devices off or putting them out of reach at least 45 minutes to an hour before bed. I would suggest doing more of this throughout the day.

#3: ORDER OUT

Order your favorite dish. Sushi from the Sushi Boat in San Francisco, Samosas and Naan or whatever is going to make you feel great. You shouldn't lift a finger... except to dial the number.

#4: GET OUT OF THE HOUSE!

If you prefer you can get some fresh air instead of ordering out. It is so easy to get distracted from your goals when sitting inside the house. You say you are going to do your kick-boxing DVD, but that strawberry cake you made last night is sitting on your counter. Stop self-sabotage before it starts by going to a place (somewhere that's not your home or office) to work on your goals.

#5: SET THE AMBIANCE

Put on your favorite iTunes playlist. I got the Love Songs album by Billie Holiday from a guy friend in grad school and I love to listen to it while cleaning, writing or trying to relax.

#6: TAKE A LONG BATH

Light a candle and take a hot, relaxing bath. I love to add Warm Vanilla Sugar Bubble Bath from Bath & Body Works or Toasted Sugar by Bodycology for a less expensive version. Stay in long enough to appreciate the relaxation but not too long – you want to avoid looking like a prune.

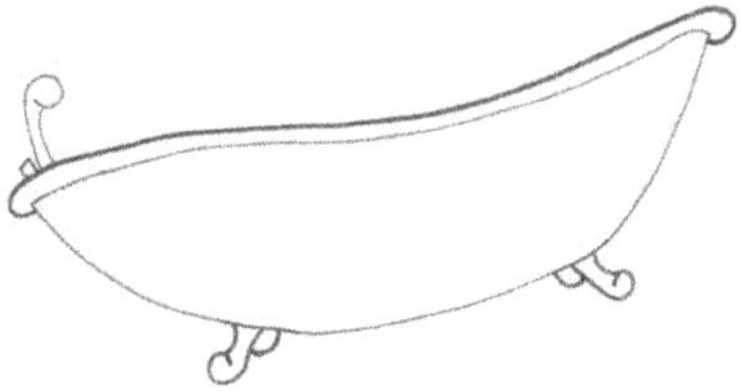

#7: NIGHT GOWN

Pull out a silk nightgown by Victoria's Secret, cotton by Ralph Lauren, or nice pajamas that make you feel relaxed and special. Go all out. It does not matter that no one else is there. Be sexy for YOU!

#8: POUR A GLASS OF WINE OR YOUR FAVORITE DRINK

Your order has arrived and you are ready for a delicious dinner. Pour yourself a glass of wine (or Shirley Temple if you prefer a non-alcoholic beverage) and enjoy! You can add a great movie to end the night, I recommend *The Devil Wears Prada*, or just enjoy the candlelight and wine while drifting off to sleep.

Being sensationally single doesn't mean that you don't want to date or marry in the future - it just means that you are content with where you are. For the most part, I don't notice being single. Well...until holiday time. I've even thought about getting a holiday boyfriend. You know, the guy friend you can take the holiday office parties. Ha!

Enjoy this time in your life. Work on you. Start that business that you've alway wanted to, volunteer, and really get to know yourself. When the time is right, Prince Charming will show up. At least that's what my grandmother told me. He has yet to show up on my door, as far as I know. I've been too busy to notice. Hope he leaves a note if he does.

DIVA RECAP:

- Singleness is a time where you should get to know you.
- Protect your happy.
- Shift your focus to something other than finding a partner. What business are you supposed to create? What book are you supposed to write? Focus on that.
- Resolve any issue from previous relationships or heartbreaks from your past.
- Evaluate your relationships.
- Pamper yourself.

7.

BLESSED & HIGHLY FAVORED.

"How are you?" I asked. She replied:
"Blessed & highly favored."

During my short time as a barista, before I was laid off a second time, I got to meet some interesting people. I'm not sure why some people have to have their coffee before they can be civil. I've had people come in to get coffee and ask me for my phone number after finding out I was a designer. Silly me. I gave this guy my number because I thought he was a potential design client only to find out he was hitting on me and had asked for another coworker's number. But when you are thinking about getting a job, networking is always on your mind. Some people take advantage of that. I was disgusted every time after that he came to get his coffee. But there was this one lady who came in. As I handed her change and a hazelnut latté, she smiled at me as I asked her how she was doing. She replied, *"blessed and highly favored"* and then began to walk away. I watched her stride out the door with an aura of happiness surrounding her. She was glowing pure radiance and I started to cry. I wanted to stop her and ask, "How do you know...how do you know you are blessed and highly favored when everything around you is pure chaos?"

I wanted the answer. In fact, I needed it. I was feeling empty and I'm not sure what her life was like at the time of our short exchange, but mine was pure chaos. I was suffocating. The barista job that I was working would come to an end right before Thanksgiving. It was holiday season, and I got laid off. Her latté was one of the last coffees I made, and I did not get the chance to ask her my question.

My spirit was crying out for peace in the midst of chaos. I wanted to know how to achieve this state of being during any season, storm, or situation in my life. I even wrote a blog post titled, "Do Not Let Your Happenings Ruin Your

Happiness." But the daggers that were being pierced into my side from every direction were far too many and caused me to lose sight of the post that I wrote with my own keyboard.

How can I be "blessed and highly favored" when nothing I touch seems to be bearing good fruit? Job applications are falling on deaf ears, student loans are due, I was having family issues, and a lot of my relationships were changing.

'Where is my peace, Lord?' I was internally calling out for help. I felt like Jill Scott's character Sheila in *Why Did I Get Married?* when she said that she felt as if the Lord had given up on her. I would lay in my bed for hours at night crying and calling out, *"Please don't give up on me...fill me. I am so empty."*

My father always told me that I was born under a star. I can't say for sure when he started telling me this but I know that I've heard it for years. Well, I felt like that star had fallen and I was being stripped of the worth that I had just recently taken back from my childhood pain. Then, one night during one of my midnight cries, I started to rethink what my worth was tied to. Was my worth only tied to my bank account? Was my worth tied to someone else's vision of me? Was my worth tied to society's view of success? Or was my worth tied to the way God saw me?

How do you define your worth? How do you define success? Far more important than becoming financially wealthy is becoming spiritually wealthy. If you place your worth in the way God sees you, then when your materials are stripped from you, your self-image will still stand firm because it was not tied to those materials in the first place. Or when you get rejected your self-esteem won't shake because its not God who is rejecting you. Your purpose and worth will not be locked up in man.

So what I was out of work? The Lord made sure my rent was paid. I had to be humble in these circumstances and ask for help. I'm an only child and a Daddy's girl, so people often thought that my parents were taking care of me. But I'm a very independent spirit and I get a lot of pride from taking care of myself and achieving my goals. What I learned during this season is that sometimes you will be put into situations where the only thing you can say is, "help me." You will get to a point where you are comfortable saying it because your life depends on it. My grandmother sent me money to pay my rent one month. While I was very grateful, I was also very upset. I wanted to be at a point in my life (even though I was in my mid 20s) to take care of my grandmother. I wanted to send her money, not the other way around. But everything has a season. And it was mine to go through this.

So what I had student loans due? He made sure they were deferred. I would get the calls and would not answer them. Not because I didn't want to, but because I couldn't. Everything was coming at me so quickly and bills were piling up. If I got one more call I wasn't going to be able to handle it mentally. The calls I did pick up were often emotional. *"It would give me nothing but great joy to pay these student loans off,"* I would tell them. That was true. But I could barely afford to pay attention.

So what I had to cut back on some of the things I loved to do? He blessed my friends to be able to treat me every now and then. I have great friends and I'm thankful for that. These friends would often invite me out and treat me to dinner. I was and am grateful for them helping me get through. It was very humbling for me to be in that position. I would prefer to treat my friends and would think nothing of it. But allowing someone to bless you when you cannot bless them back is a very humbling experience. One that I will never forget.

And then I realized what it means to be "blessed and highly favored." It is the ability that God gives you to go on in spite of your circumstance. Every day I was alive, I was able to put in another application. Each day, despite the bottom line on my checkbook, I was able to pray, cry, laugh and scream, and I made it through. I was able to go through that season so that I could get to the next one.

Perhaps my father was right, I was born under a star. This star was placed in the heavens especially to shine on me.

Take some time to look at the stars tonight. The star that is beaming brightly and lighting the path is yours. Though the night fog may cover it, occasionally hindering the light from guiding your path, it is still yours.

God never gave up on me and He will never give up on you. He will never leave. But He will teach us during times of trouble the lessons we need to make it through this life. He used this opportunity to teach me that even in a storm, I am blessed and highly favored. *What is He teaching you?*

DIVA RECAP:

- Your self worth shouldn't be tied to your net worth.
- Live in YOUR season.
- Be HUMBLE.
- You are blessed and highly favored.

8.

WHAT TYPE OF FRIEND ARE YOU?

I was watching a YouTube clip one day of Bishop TD Jakes preaching about the three different types of people that one will interact with: Confidants, Constituents, and Comrades[7]. I love the way he explained the meaning behind each of them.

As he explained them, a confidant is a person who is for you. This person is someone who will mentor you and be there for you whether you are right or wrong, up or down. If you have a few confidants, then you are a blessed person. A constituent is someone who is just with you as long as you stand together. As long as you are for what they are for they will walk with you. But if someone else comes along who can further their agenda, they will leave. And lastly, comrades. A comrade is someone who is against what you are against. They will team up with you to fight a greater battle but when the victory is won, they too will leave you.

I love how he spoke about these types of people. They

apply not only to friendships but also to coworkers and relationships.

In kindergarten, it was easy to make friends. You simply went out to the playground, found someone you liked and asked them to be your friend. If you had a tiff, it only lasted about 20 minutes and then you were friends again. If only friendships were this easy as an adult.

Many of us have considered people friends or gotten into relationships too soon. We mistake an initial connection as something that will last a lifetime and then when the friendship or relationship is over, we are devastated. In adult life, being a friend has its rules. A true friend should have their friend's best interest close to their heart. I mean, why would anyone want a friend that they cannot trust with their true feelings?

Sure, developing a friendship takes time and you want to get to know a persons character completely. Building a successful friendship takes years — not months or weeks. Pay attention to a person's moral value. That will be a key component in how they will treat you as a friend. In my experience, people will come into your life for three purposes: a reason, a season or a lifetime. I have been blessed with some great lessons from people who came into my life through one or more of these categories.

A REASON

The people that come into your life for a reason are only there to teach you something or help you learn a lesson. There may not be a terrible break from these people. It's just that when their time in your life is over they move on.

Rita was a beautiful and petite Indian girl I met during a summer program called Aim High. We must have been about 11 or 12 years old when we met each other at Roosevelt High School in San Francisco. We quickly became friends, and days later I was emulating her style.

I remember being infatuated with her signature style: pointed-toe flats with perfectly fitted jeans and a cardigan-like shirt. I quickly went home and pulled a pair of white pointed-toe flats out of my closet and paired them with jeans also. It's true that imitation is a form of flattery. It was another example of me trying to find my identity.

The day that our summer program ended, we had a cultural celebration. Students brought dishes from their culture and some, including Rita, performed traditional dances. I can still hear the music that Rita danced to... Humma, Humma, Humma, Eh...Eh, Humma.

Rita, like Angela, taught me about a culture that was different than mine. She taught me about style. But we were only friends for that reason. After Aim High I never heard from her again. But the affect she had on my life still stands firm.

A SEASON

People who come in your life for a season tend to stay longer than people who come in for a reason. By seasons, I'm not talking about Fall, Winter, Spring and Summer. I'm talking about spiritual seasons that are meant to groom you and prepare you for the next season in your life.

I've talked about Annie several times in this book. She is an example of a seasonal person in my life. During my two middle school years in San Francisco, Annie was instrumental in showing me what grace and kindness looked like. My memories of her are always fun and her smile is one I will always remember. She helped me through a lot of situations ones I remember and some I'm sure I've forgotten. I tried to stay in touch with her when I moved to Florida, but that didn't work out as I had hoped. When I got back to California almost a decade later I reached out but far too much time had passed for us to reconnect. I am forever grateful for her season in my life because it helped me make it to my next season.

A LIFETIME

Lifetime people are ones who you will develop a solid bond with that lasts throughout all seasons of your life. These people will most likely makeup the core of your inner circle. Lifetime people can also be people whom had a profound affect on your life whether or not they are still alive.

I met Angela in the fifth grade when I moved to California. We lived in a red brick duplex on the Presidio and Angela's family shared the duplex with us. She was a very petite Korean girl with round cheeks. I remember being in awe of her because she was different, she was something that I had never seen before. Meeting her was one of the first times that I remember being introduced to a culture other than my own.

Her mother became my Emo (Korean for Aunt) and also taught me a bit about Korean culture. We were both military brats and only children so we had a lot in common. We got in arguments as most friends do. When I moved away to Florida Angie got to stay and finish eighth grade (which was the last grade in our middle school) before moving to Colorado. We stayed in touch for years through writing letters and then we fell out of touch. We both wanted to go back to California so when I moved back I hunted for her number to see if she too had made it back to California.

Emo Christine (Angie's mom) picked up the phone.

"Hi Emo, how are you?"

I was so excited that I don't think I let her finish before saying,

"It's Crystal (I was just Crystal then), can I speak to Angie."

After a pause she started crying.

"I thought you knew. Angie died."

What??!! No I didn't know. I knew we stopped writing but I wasn't quite sure if it was me who stopped responding or if life just got in the way.

"She died in a car accident. Her fault."

I couldn't breathe. Angie's culture had become my culture. She shared that with me at a young age. I can't explain to you how Korean historical culture and cuisine has a place in my heart. I had lost contact with her. Emo asked me a few questions about being married or single and she told me that I could call anytime. I honestly haven't. I was so embarrassed that I was such a bad friend that I didn't even know that she had died that I couldn't bring myself to pick up that phone again.

Rest in Peace Angela Y. Fanello (1983-2003) and Thank you for sharing your culture with me.

Now that you have an idea of what it means to have a reason, season and lifetime friend, think about your relationships and start listing your friends in these categories. Are there some friendships/relationships that you are holding on to but should let go of because they are only to be in your life for a reason? Are there seasonal friends whose season in your life is over? Are there lifetime friendships/relationships that you need to solidify?

DIVA RECAP:

- Friendships/Relationships come into your life for a reason, season or lifetime. Don't mislabel people.
- Not all people who leave your life, leave because of a bad breakup. Sometimes their reason or season with you is over.
- Evaluate yourself as a friend. How you treat people will mirror how they treat you.
- Spend time with the friends you have. Make the time to stay in touch. Life is short.

9.

WHAT A DIVA'S STYLE SPEAKS FOR HERSELF.

Keep Your Heels, Head & Standards High
~Coco Chanel

I remember in my teens being teased for having a unique style. I had a style of which my peers did not understand. But it was mine. I was wearing Nine West flats in middle school while the other girls were wearing baggy jeans and Nike tennis shoes. They told me that I could not match and my clothes were ugly. You see, even then I knew that no one should be too matchy-matchy, and I believed everyone should take risks in their style. I was into sophistication and the risks that I took early on in life are the ones that shape my style to this very day.

When you are younger, your style will most likely be influenced by your mother or mother-figure. This can be a positive or negative fact. For me, my mother was into all things fashion, including keeping a nicely decorated home.

As her clothing tastes matured, mine did also. But your true style comes when you begin choosing and buying your own clothes. Do you stay within your mother's ideal vision of your style or do you begin to experiment?

I experimented. It will only stick if you find your style. This is especially important for the young divas who don't quite know what kind of image they want to project through their clothes, hair and overall look.

When I watch the current teen dramas and news about young women and their battle with beauty, I feel sorry that they feel they have to keep up with what society says is the ideal look or weight. Young women are suffering from bulimia and going on crash diets to appease whom?

The idea of young women going on crash diets seems outrageous to me. However, I also spoke of crash dieting before school started. The pages of my young diary remind me that I had singleness of mind about the issue. If it didn't work, I said, I was not going to school. There is even mention of bringing an extra bag of clothes to change into so that I could change out of my "dull" clothes. Even though this diary entry was from middle school I remember vividly in high school changing on the bus. My friend had given me this cute Tommy Hilfiger outfit that was a short mini skirt and matching top combination. My mom told me that I couldn't wear it because it was too short. So I snuck it in my backpack and changed in to it on the bus. I for sure turned heads but not for the right reasons. I had to keep pulling the skirt down so that it would be decent. As I look back on it, I see my mom was right. But I just wanted to feel "liked."

Who was I trying to impress, and why?

This is what our young women are going through behind closed doors, in their beds at night, and between the pages of their young diaries. They are struggling to define themselves in a world where self-esteem is measured by how close you look to a magazine cover girl.

THE BEGINNINGS OF STYLE.

During my early teenage years I became familiar with brands such as COACH, Ralph Lauren, Dooney & Burke, Old Navy and of course the teenage stores such as Charlotte Rousse and Express. My first job was at Sears, and with the encouragement of the 20-percent discount, my shopping career began there. I worked there for three years until I started my undergraduate years in college.

As I matured, so did my choice in brands. Some of this fashion maturity came as a necessity. As I got older, my body went through many changes and the jeans I once wore no longer suited my shape. Enter Express jeans: perfect for my college budget, Express jeans had the perfect fit. Thank goodness for that perfectly fit jean. Between Express and Old Navy I was in blue-jean heaven. And since jeans were what I wore a lot in college, it was important to have brands that were wallet-friendly.

Now almost 15 years later, my taste in jeans have evolved. Jeans are still a staple in my wardrobe because I work for a high tech company in Silicon Valley. Brands like Farrah, H&M, Lauren Conrad, Armani Exchange, and Just Black have entered my closet.

My mother also had a hand in helping me develop my style. When she would discover new brands she liked, I would buy those brands as well. We didn't share clothes, but I was definitely paying attention to what she bought and why. And I still do.

Going to college was another fashion eye opener. There was an extreme amount of diversity in the way women dressed at my college. I went to Florida A&M University and most of the women I knew dressed well when they went to class including wearing heels on those hills.

I learned a great deal from just watching people. It was a trend when I was in college to wear African-style head wraps. Even though I can say now that this isn't much of my style, I still experimented with it. You have to try new things to know if you truly like them or not.

DIVA'S STYLE RULES.

1. Try New Things - Get comfortable enough with your style to be confident but never get comfortable enough to be complacent. Experiment with new styles and try things on that you think you would never wear. When you find something you like that is not something you would traditionally wear, buy it. Rock it with confidence and watch heads turn.

2. Get Some Go-To Jeans - Find a pair of jeans that you cannot live without. I still love Express Jeans. But my absolute favorite jeans now are a pair I found through my

StitchFix by Just Black.

3. *Be Overall Classic, Not Trendy* - It's cool to have a few trendy pieces in your wardrobe but overall your look should be classic. I'm not necessarily talking about that Jackie O look, but more about a look that you can sustain over time. Buy pieces that you can wear five to seven years from now. That is classic no matter how you categorize your style.

4. *A Nice Blazer* - Invest in one. I adore Ralph Lauren blazers for the very reason I mentioned in No. 3. I've had most of the RL blazers I own for years and they are always in style. His brand has mastered the classic blazer. You can wear a blazer over a nice dress for a party look or over a t-shirt and jeans for a casual tech look.

5. *On Trend* - While you shouldn't look at your wardrobe and realize that it is filled with only trendy pieces, it doesn't hurt to mix in a few trends to spice up your classic style. I'm loving leopard right now. The leopard trend comes and goes

so ideally when this trend goes away in a year or so, I can tuck my pieces in the back of my closet and pull them out when the trend resurfaces. I've always loved leopard whether its in season or not. In high school art class I had a pink leopard bag that I carried my books in. Yes. Pink Leopard.

6. *Break the Rules* - Now that I've given you some of my rules for style, break them. Make up your own and have fun doing it.

DEVELOPING STYLE.

Now I must warn you, when you are developing your style people will voice their opinions whether you want them to or not and you will have some fashion faux pas. But you must remain strong and comfortable in your choices and learn from your mistakes. Yes, there can be fashion mistakes. Not everything that looks good on the hanger will look good on you. You have to know your body shape and dress it accordingly. The opinions that people will voice may hurt you but some of them (especially people who are close to you and come from a place of love) can be helpful.

I have a sorority sister who I love to go shopping with. We can both give each other honest opinions about what looks good on our body types. Sometimes we disagree with the opinion of one another and get the clothing item anyway. But over the last almost decade we have developed a honest opinion about each other's style not only based on what we like but also what we know the other person will like.

For a Diva, paying attention to art and fashion can be a full-time job. Art is everywhere and in everything. It is what you wear, what you see around you...everything. From the mirror in the bathroom, the pictures you hang on the wall and the clothes you choose to wear, a woman – especially a Diva – is a high end painting walking. People will notice you when you stroll down the street.

Of course, we all have physical flaws and we should acknowledge that. Work on your flaws while you accentuate your positive attributes. For example, I love to eat bread. Those carbs have gone to my stomach and thighs. I struggle with my stomach hanging over my pants a bit. This I would say is my biggest physical flaw besides my adult acne. But I still love myself and appreciate where I am. However, I don't want to stay where I am when it can be easily fixed by going to the gym and cutting back on eating a 24 count of Hawaiian Bread Rolls. Denying that my stomach is hanging over my jeans will do nothing for me.

While I was in high school, I began wearing hazel contacts and this continued throughout my college career. It became a part of my signature style, but it came from a place of insecurity. You never saw me in my glasses. It was because I didn't feel beautiful if I was not wearing them. When I started graduate school at San Francisco State University, I said enough is enough. I need to take full control of my self esteem so I ditched the hazel contacts and haven't looked back. While dying your hair or wearing extensions, wearing contacts and makeup and fancy fabulous clothing can help your look, it cannot fix how you feel about yourself. So if you look in the mirror without all of these things and do not consider yourself beautiful, then we have work to do on your self esteem.

There is a quote I read in Nina Garcia's book, *The Little Black Book of Style*[8], that speaks to me when it comes to style and beauty.

> "Nothing makes a woman more beautiful
> than the belief that she is beautiful."
> ~Sophia Loren

When you truly are in touch with your internal beauty, it

radiates in everything that you do. There is a quiet confidence that I admire in women who believe in themselves. They don't have to sell you their beauty, you can see it when they walk in the room. Its not pushy or obnoxious but it smacks you in the face in a humble and graceful way. This is the type of woman we should aim to become if we are not already.

STYLE EXERCISE #1

- Who are some of the women that you admire for their internal beauty? Try to think of some of the women who are in your life not just celebrities. Write them down.
- Why do you admire these women? Make a list.
- If there is something about their style that you would like to incorporate into yours, ask them to help you.
- Who are your celebrity style icons?
- What do your celebrity style icons have in common

with the other women in your life that you admire?

BUDGETING STYLE.

Shopping is ingrained in our culture. For most of us, shopping makes us happy. It's retail therapy and no matter how many figures you have in your bank account, you want to do what makes you happy. You have to be smart about your purchases and you have to work within your budget. While you can look at celebrities for style inspiration, if you don't have celebrity money then you will have to find a look for less. I'm a firm believer in looking your best and living in your season. So if you are on a tight budget, look at places like Ross, Target, TJ Maxx, and outlet stores.

When you land a better job that affords you to shop a bit more then try stores like Macy's, Nordstrom, COACH, and Ralph Lauren. And when you are blessed and land your dream job then venture out into the world of Manolo

Blahnik, Jimmy Choo and Chanel. How wonderful would that be? I am still dreaming of having my first Carrie Bradshaw moment in a pair of Manolo Blahnik shoes.

Blazers, jeans, winter coats, furs, high-heels, flats, handbags, earrings, necklaces, bracelets, sculptures, paintings – whatever your go-to purchase is, it must be designer. Of course, the designer that you choose must fit your lifestyle and be one that comes from your style and not what comes from television. Don't get caught up with the prestige of having a certain designer bag. Get the bag that you like. Not everything with an expensive price tag is quality and not everything that is on sale is cheap. Be stylish but be you.

DIVA RECAP:

- Your style is about you and what you like. Don't try to keep up with the Joneses or your favorite celebrity. You are not the Joneses.
- Experiment with different styles. You never know what you may find.
- Great style can develop over time. So live in your season. Budget your style.
- Break the rules. Be stylish and smart.
- Change the things you don't like about your style or your physical appearance. But be confident while you are doing it. Don't do it for someone else or to look like a model on the cover of a major magazine. Most of that is Photoshop anyway.

10.

A DIVA'S PRESENCE.

The power of presence is amazing. We have all seen that woman who walks into a room with such confidence and poise and we have all wanted to be that woman. What is her story? How did she become a vessel full of confidence?

Behind her model-esque walk, Crest-whitened smile and intelligent conversation, you may find a person who years ago was just like you. And the only difference between the two of you is experience.

While there is no easy answer, getting in touch with your vulnerabilities is the perfect start. So many times as women we are afraid of what people might think about us. Our minds are constantly filling our hearts with insecurities. Forget this idea of being afraid! Embrace your weaknesses and use them as opportunities for growth.

The next time you see that woman walk into a room, be confident enough to ask her, *"Where does your ______ (whatever you admire her for) presence come from?"* You never know where this may lead you: A great cup of tea with a new friend, shopping in Venice, or front row at a life-changing event that teaches you something about yourself.

Life-changing events come in different ways and sometimes they are just a minute long connection with a person that changes your life. This chapter is inspired by one of those events for me. I was laid off and at the beginning of a rough season in my life and I just got back from spending two months in Florida (I moved to Florida from California to live with my parents). Due to some family issues, I landed back in California pretty quickly. I felt alone and a mess. I joined a group called Girls in Tech and went to one of their first events that I can remember. It was Sarah Lacy's book signing. I managed to scrape up the $20 to buy the book and gain entry to the event. I walked up this amazingly steep hill and was sweating profusely. As soon as I paid my admission, I bought a soda at the bar and sat down by myself. I was just proud that I made it. One lady at the bar approached me and must have noticed how anxious I was.

"It's your first time at one of these isn't it?" she asked.

I smiled as I often do when I don't want to be rude and assume that someone wants to shoot another dagger in my already hurting side. But her statement did sting a bit. She left and I found another seat at a table. Two ladies came up to me and started talking. I'm still so thankful for both of them. They made my time at the event a bit less awkward. By this time I was starting to sweat less and calm down. I found out that the women I was speaking with were having similar issues. The economy was tough and I wasn't in that alone.

It was time for the talk to begin so we quickly moved to the other section of the bar to get front row seats. Sarah began to talk and one of the best things I remember was her saying that she may take her shoes off during the talk. Rock on! Sometimes high heels do hurt. Why stand there giving an hour long speech in a room full of women and be in pain? A few seconds later the beautiful tall blonde woman sitting in front of me asked Sarah:

"Where do you get your presence from?"

I honestly can't remember Sarah's answer. But the lady in front of me went on to say how she is a speech coach and she guides people in developing an on-stage presence. I was attracted to this woman. No not in the "I want to date you" sense. But in the divine connection sense. I knew that I would one day be publishing books and preparing for talks. But that wasn't my time. So I rummaged up enough courage to ask for her card. I tapped her gently on the shoulder and said,

"Can I have your card?"

She smiled, handed it to me and then told me about a group workshop she was having and there were a few spots left. Instantly I thought to myself, I cannot afford that. Not now. My face must have said it all because just then the lady, whom I now know as Bronwyn, said: *"You know what? Come and be my guest."*

I could have let a tear drop at that moment. But I believe I kept it together. I said thank you and put the card in my purse. I'll be honest and say that I struggled a bit whether to take her up on this offer. God was teaching me about being humble. How can you need help and be so afraid to accept it once it is offered to you? I realized that by asking her for her card and accepting her offer to be a guest at her workshop, I was already taking steps toward owning my presence.

I attended Bronwyn's workshop that she held with another powerful woman, Kristine. I am so grateful that I didn't let pride get in the way of my blessing. There was so much knowledge shared in that workshop. While it was a struggle getting there (I got lost and ended up super late), I still remember the exercises being a tough challenge for me to get through. They helped me to realize that it is confidence and lots of practice that will help you get through public speaking.

DIVA RECAP:

- Don't be afraid to own your presence.
- Be you and embrace whatever that YOU is.
- Ask for help when you need it and be willing to accept help that is offered. You never know what blessing is behind your humbleness.

11.
EMOTIONAL ROLLER COASTER.

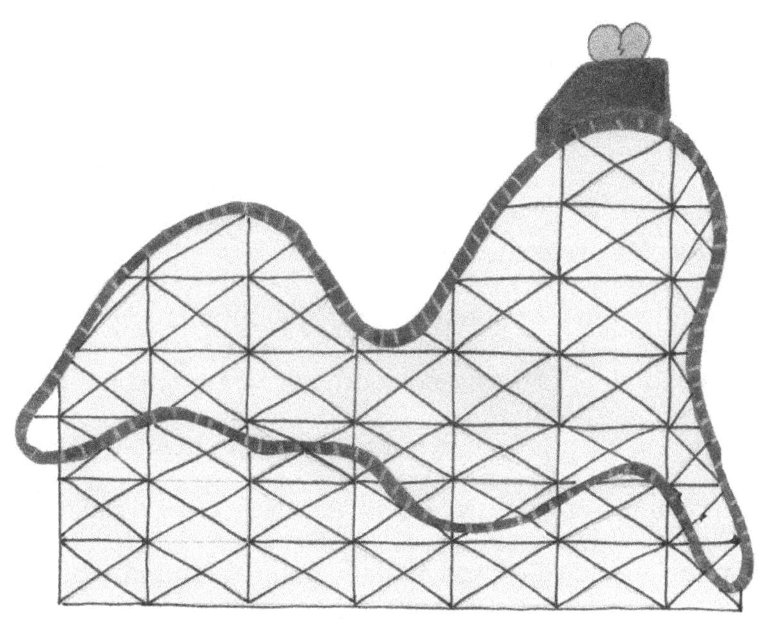

I am grateful for the lessons I've learned throughout emotional seasons in my life and I must say that remembering to keep mentally centered was the most important. You cannot help anyone — including yourself — until you are relaxed and in control of your life.

In 2008, I was at the tale end of a phenomenal — yet short — design internship. Although I was hoping that the internship would transition into an entry-level position, it did not. The director previously let me know that the company was unable to hire until they received some new clients. But I remained optimistic.

Months and hundreds of résumé submissions later, I began to panic. Having no source of steady income was a new thing for me. I could not recall ever being in a position where bills were getting behind and there was no safety net. My optimism grew scarce and the reality of the situation set in.

In October 2008, my economic situation moved me back to my parents' home in Florida at the age of 25. I felt like a failure. On my 3,000-mile drive back to Florida from California, I tried desperately to make sense of my life and see the light at the end of the tunnel. That light was dim if it was shining at all.

My first month and a half back in Florida I stayed cooped up in my room with no energy or motivation to get out of bed. I rarely answered phone calls and found myself spiraling back into depression. I dreaded falling back into the depressed state that once consumed my childhood years.

The health of my emotions and spirit became my priority. I prayed more and started to pick up my phone calls. I reconnected with old friends and circumstances had me on my way back to California in late January 2009. It was during my first months back in San Francisco that I realized I am not alone. A plethora of men and women, regardless of age or original income, were going through the same transitions in life. This gave me great comfort and provided me the opportunity for growth.

Here are a few tips I used to stay mentally fit during the economic downturn:

#1: EMBRACE SOLITUDE.

Pray, meditate, or do some form of relaxation at least 15 minutes a day. Even watching your favorite television show will work.

I had to do anything that would get my mind off being depressed even if it was for a few minutes. I love historical Korean dramas and would often have a drama marathon while in bed. It kept my mind distracted from my current situation. Prayer was also a part of healing. I would cry out to God and my prayers became more like talks. When I couldn't cry anymore or talk anymore I went back to my historical dramas. I did anything to get me through to the next day. It was difficult and there were times I didn't think I was going to make it to the next day. But God.

#2: ASK FOR HELP.

Easier said than done, but very effective. Reach out to people in your network; they may provide you with great resources and give you time-tested advice. Independent doesn't mean you will never need to ask for help.

Sometimes I didn't have to reach out. Because I was honest about what I was going through some people would reach out to me. When I returned from Florida one of my sorority sisters paid for me to attend the Girls in Tech Catalyst Conference. It was a great way for me to spend two days geeking out on technology with women in technology and not worrying too much about my home life.

#3: TALK TO A THERAPIST.

If you think you are suffering from depression, let a trained therapist help. It can be a scary and dangerous time when going through depression alone.

I am an advocate for doing what works for you. I went to therapy for a while when I was in high school. While it did not work for me at the time, I believe that it still does work for some people. I know a few people who have received counseling and it has done wonders for them. If you are not comfortable going alone bring a trusted friend with you. It was two of my best friends that suggested that I go in high school. I appreciate and love them for being honest and loving me enough to want me to get help.

#4: CREATE AN EXERCISE ROUTINE.

Try to go a few times a week for 1-2 hours. It can release pent-up energy and clear congested thoughts.

When I wasn't praying and watching Korean dramas, I did go to the gym in my apartment building. It was another outlet for me. I knew that I was going through really tough times when I cried in the gym during my time on the treadmill. It was a small gym, and I was the only one in there, so I just let it out. Honestly, even if someone else was in the gym, I would have cried to my heart's content anyway. Life will take you some places and you cannot be afraid of letting out your emotions in front of people. Who cares? This is about you getting through.

#5: READ AN ENCOURAGING BLOG.

Of course I recommend TheDivaInc.com. The life lessons and encouragement from women with myriad experiences will help you know that you are not alone and there is more to being a Diva than appearances.

I started TheDivaInc.com as a personal blog during

one of the roughest times in my life. It was my way of getting out my emotions and trying to connect with other women who were going through similar things and needed encouragement. Even though I was spiraling down to rock bottom, I wanted to give whatever encouraging words I had left in me to someone who was struggling more than me.

#6: BE FREE.

Look for fun free events around your neighborhood. You will have a blast and not have to feel guilty about the bill.

When finances are strapped you learn to find creative ways to start enjoying life. Especially when you want to live. I found out that this super high end massage place on the Presidio was giving free massages to people who were unemployed. I signed up immediately. From there I spoke to a few women who were also unemployed and they told me about a free blow out from another high end salon in Union

Square. You bet I signed up. I didn't just think of these events as free but I thought of them as little bread crumb blessings God was giving me to lead me out of despair and into greater blessings.

#7: GO OUT.

Getting out of the house is key during tough seasons in your life. Take a walk on the beach, go to your local coffee shop or just sit on the curb. When you are cooped up in your house, you are more likely to stay in your emotional state.

I got tired of staying in the bed and house all the time. But I was afraid to go out because even a cup of tea costs money. So what would I do outside when I had to be super budget conscious? I had to budget nothing and turn it into rent money and grocery money. But I was ignoring the blessings that were all around me. I lived in walking distance from the beach. What was I thinking to be in the house all the time?

So to get out, I began walking to the beach. It was hard at first to have the energy to get out of the bed and make the trek to the beach. But as days passed (I tried to go every day), it became easier.

#8: CREATE SOMETHING.

Not only is art a form of expression but it is also a great stress reliever. Pick up a pencil, paper and/or paint. Have fun.

I did a bit of sketching while I was on the beach sometimes. I already had the supplies since I had two degrees in design so it didn't cost me anything to pick up my sketch pad and pencils and draw something. Anything. Just create something because I could. Look online for DIY projects and try to find something that you can do that doesn't require you to buy anything that you don't already own.

#9: LAUGH.

Do not be too engulfed in your job, life, family problems, that you forget to laugh. Laughing is a natural way of lifting your spirit.

Even if you are at rock bottom, there is always something to laugh at or smile about. Find that thing and smile.

#10: MAKE A LIST.

Start thinking about what you want to change and write it down. Hang the list on your bathroom mirror and read your goals every morning. It is also good to write down your favorite inspirational quote.

I'm finding more and more that it is so important to write your goals down. Don't type it. Write it in your own handwriting. Allow yourself to dream and not be limited. I am a fan of The Day Designer Planner by Whitney English and The Purposeful Planner by Corie Clark. Everything gets written down...everything. Google these products. Thank me later.

DIVA RECAP:

- Life is a roller coaster. Strap up and enjoy the ride.
- You WILL make it through. Just keep going through. Don't stop and take up residence in a tough situation. Speak it and believe it.
- Protect your mental health.
- Get the help you need, laugh and make time to see even the smallest of blessings.

12.
MAKING A WAY OUT OF NO WAY.

All of my experiences, from selling t-shirts and recruiting insurance salespeople, to passing out on my floor crying over my situation and lack of finances the last few years, have taught me so much about who I am. One other thing they taught me is that the person who came up with the mini meal for McDonald's is a genius. With my budget dwindling, I had stopped spending money on wants and barely could spend them on needs. When I was in a pinch, the McDonald's mini-meal came to the rescue!

I had it figured out that I could get one mini-meal ($3.27) a day. This beat buying groceries because it kept me from spending way more upfront. If I got the mini-meal and I needed something the next day I might still have money for it. Yes...times were that hard. I planned out every penny I spent and every meal I ate to allow me to have some "extra" cash on hand for emergencies. Sure, if the emergency had cost over $20 at any given time, I would have been out of luck. If I needed to use some of that cash on hand cash, I would cut out the mini-meal and wouldn't eat that day.

Things were tight. I'm not going to put on any airs about that. I did what I thought was best in the moment to survive. I never truly went hungry and always seemed to have enough. Friends would occasionally take me out to eat and I even gained weight. Well, the weight part is a not-so-good side effect. Not only was the price of the mini-meal (not to mention they had four choices) appealing, but the convenience of it. There was a McDonald's right down the street from the apartment in Emeryville I had moved to. I moved from San Francisco to Emeryville to avoid having to move back to Florida. I was hoping that the reduction in rent wold hold me over until one of the jobs I had been doing would provide me steady income to live. But I was afraid to leave my apartment if it got too dark, and my boyfriend at the time got approached by drug dealers when he pulled up in his BMW. Even when I moved out of that apartment and later found myself back in San Francisco, McDonald's was everywhere.

While working as a barista I could use my tips for things like mini-meals and gas. When things got much better, I still found myself frequenting the mini-meal much more than I would care to admit. I could afford better, but I had spent a few years creating a habit that was no longer necessary, but difficult to break.

"Make it Work!"
- Tim Gunn, Project Runway

Although Tim Gunn's quote is in reference to the designers on Project Runway, it sums up what Divas do. We make it work! It is what we do during tough times when we are presented with decisions about whether we can afford to eat. Somehow, we not only manage to feed our children, we eat as well. Believe me, my darling divas, I look back on those times and wonder what I would do if I had children to take care of, and then I think of Divas like some of you who are mothers struggling to feed your children. We are grandmothers filling in the gap and young women who have yet to embark on any struggle of this nature. Whether we survive on sheer determination to make ends meet or the resourcefulness of a mini-meal as an eating plan, we make it work. I give respect to those mothers, thanks to those grandmothers and hopefully with this book will educate and prepare those young women for these challenges.

The key is survival. Sure, some may have made different choices than I. But one option that we all have in common is the choice to survive.

DIVA RECAP:

- As long as you are not hurting people or yourself and doing anything illegal, do what you have to within reason to survive.
- Make the best decision you can in your circumstances. You may make a different decision if given the choice but sometimes you don't have a choice. Do the best you can to get through. Some seasons are supposed to hurt. But don't let them break you.

13.
BOUNCING BACK MEANS HITTING THE BOTTOM.

A few years ago when the economy was beginning to take a downfall, I was presented with an amazing opportunity to intern at an ad agency in Sausalito. It was going to be a short internship but I was hoping that it would turn into an entry-level position. I quit my job at Kinko's to take this internship, stepping out on faith that it would turn into something greater. The internship ended and I was left jobless.

I only had a small amount of money saved and a few credit cards that I maxed out to keep me sheltered and fed. My grandmother was instrumental in helping me survive for the next few months. And while I was grateful for all of her help, encouragement and prayers, I wanted to be in a position to help her. I was no where near that point and couldn't afford to pay attention.

I put out my résumé everywhere and took every small design job I could. As a matter of fact, if you look in your email, you may have a copy of my résumé. Ha! Every job site I could think of had a copy of my résumé and skills set. At the advice of my grandmother, I worked with a recruiting firm in Oakland. The name of the firm escapes my memory, but even with my master's degree in industrial arts, they were unable to place me. Or at least they did not call me back. All my friends and sisters from my church were looking into possibilities for me, but nothing was coming into fruition.

Then – finally – there was a break!

I was contacted for a marketing position I applied for through one of the job sites. This position was advertised as entry-level with upward mobility. Thank you, Jesus! I immediately set up an interview with them. I pulled out my black knee-long skirt, gold camisole, blue Ralph Lauren signature blazer, topped off with my black COACH pumps. I was going to land this job for sure and I was taking no prisoners. I needed a job for the money, of course, but also because sitting around the house was getting more depressing day by day.

I drove my gold Pontiac Sunfire with its gas tank very close to E from San Francisco to Hayward, California. As I approached the location I saw the parking lot filled with cars. I maneuvered my car into a spot and jumped out. Résumé finely printed on cream linen paper, I was designed to get noticed. This was a make-or-break moment for me. I walked up to the receptionist's desk and said,

"I'm here for my interview."

She handed me a piece of paper and asked me to have a seat and fill it out.

"No problem!"

Once I sat down, I looked up for a moment only to see between 50 and 75 people suited up in their interview best. Interviewees were coming in and out of the offices on a 10 minute or so rotation. What?! How many positions do they have available?, I wondered. Was everyone going for my position? I started to work myself up in a fit. My heart started racing. I needed a job and I could guarantee these people did, too. They were in it to win it just as much as I was.

My name got called and I jolted out of my seat. The man interviewing me asked when I could come back for a second interview. I set it up for the next day or so. 'Woo-hoo! A second interview! I'm headed for greatness now!' I thought to myself. The second interview was a trial interview. During this time you spent a full day working with your group selling. Wait...What? I thought this was a marketing position. You know where I take all of the analysis and research and come up with a strategy to market a product-the print materials, web copy, you know – marketing.

This is when I realized I had been bamboozled. The exceptionally written job description on that job search site left out the part where I would be selling t-shirts outside of Walgreens. Yes, my dear Divas, yours truly sold t-shirts outside of Walgreens, Lucky's and a few other places. Did I mention that it was mid- summer when I was doing this job? That day I went to my then boyfriend's house and told him what the job was really like. He hugged me tightly and when I looked up at him he was crying. He said something like,

"I'm so hurt for you."

Yes. It was that bad my boyfriend (who was 16 years older than me) cried because he knew I had been duped.

I decided after that second interview that I would take the job. So my group member, a fellow member of the Divine Nine (made up of the four African-American sororities and five African-American Fraternities), put in a good word with the boss for me. I started the next day. I kept telling myself to be humble and appreciate that I now have a job.

The rule was that new people had to go out with the veterans for a week or so in order to get familiar with the way things worked. After the second interview and my first official day there I was anxious to get out on my own. You see, we were also on commission and when you went out with more than one person you then had to split that commission with everyone.

Let me break this down for some of my young divas reading this. We set up a table full of t-shirts, toys, water bottles, coupon books, etc. Each item had its price and commission. If we made $100 in commission and there were three people with us that meant that I only took home $33.33. I got to work around 7AM and got off around 7PM that is a 12 hour day. In essence, I only made $2.75 an hour.

By day three, a Wednesday, I had convinced the boss to let me work by myself. I wanted to see how much money I could make and if I could endure all of this. I went to the office and checked out my materials, got my table and put it in the back of my car and headed out to my site.

Once everything was set up, I began clamoring for customers to stop by my table.

"Hi, come on over," I would say, just as my trainers had taught me.

Many would pass me by and go inside the store only to come out with a Snapple or bottle of water as they felt sorry that I was in the heat suited up from head to toe in 100-degree weather. An old Indian man told me he would marry me.

"Come home with me," he said. *"I will marry you."*

Another guy stopped by my table to sell me baseball tickets. Why would I buy something when I'm trying to sell? I had the next day off, and luckily, I was headed to an interview. This time the job was selling insurance. I attended another group interview at the insurance agency only to find out I would have to pay $400 for an insurance license. The location manager and I worked something out. He needed a recruiter and I needed a job. So I signed on to be his recruiter and signed off selling t-shirts.

Friday was my last day selling t-shirts outside of Walgreens.

I very rarely leave a job without a two-weeks' notice. In fact, that was the first time I did. But under the circumstances, I think you understand. I definitely recommend giving a proper two-weeks' notice. But sometimes seasons in your life will push you so hard that you do things that you never would and reach out to people you never thought you could.

That Monday things went from bad to worse as I started my recruiter position with the insurance agency. I prepared my desk and the receptionist walked me through all of the processes I would need to know to do my job. The database I was pulling from (probably the same one that the so-called marketing firm used to find me) was outdated. The manager was paying me by the head for people I could get to come to the group interview.

It was something like $15 if they came and $25 if they became a salesperson. There were two interviews a week and 10 people could be there at once. The most I could make a week was $500, but the likelihood of everyone signing up to be an insurance salesperson after they heard it was going to be at least $400 for them to get certified was slim to none. Basically, it was costing me more to cross the Bay Bridge and come into work than what I would realistically make in my paycheck.

I arranged with the boss to work from home. That way, I saved the bridge toll and continue to provide a service that they so desperately needed. Well, so I thought. I would only come into the office two times a week when we had the group interviews. I did all my cold calls from home from my phone.

On my way in for one of the group interviews I was supposed to pick up my first check. I knocked on the receptionists door and she gave me a look and said,

"We don't have your check."

Wait...What?! I almost lost all professionalism.

"Something happened with the account that your money comes out of," she said.

Yeah, like there is no money in it, I thought to myself.

This is when I learned that talking about money and being able to demand what is rightfully yours isn't a thing to be bashful about. People and companies will use you. Some incidentally; they may be struggling and just plain in over their heads. But ultimately, you have to feel comfortable speaking up for yourself when it comes to money.

I immediately knocked on the director's door and inquired about my check. He gave me some spiel about how even I knew it was not working out:

"You even said yourself it costs you more to come into work than what you are making," he said to me, while sitting behind his cushy desk.

Unbeknownst to him, the receptionist had already told me the truth and before I knew it I blurted out,

"Really, I was under the impression that there were not enough funds in the account my money comes out of for you to pay me. That is why my check isn't here."

He looked a little embarrassed and quickly wrote me out a check. I took the check to his bank and cashed it. It wasn't a hefty check, only $100 or so. But in the situation I was in, I needed every penny.

It's funny when I think about all of this now. I couldn't see the lesson God was trying to teach me then and I see it now. He was teaching me about money matters. How many people, women especially, keep quiet when they are not paid accurately and don't negotiate their salary like they should. It is my wish that this chapter will teach you to get comfortable with money and money matters.

This was the first time someone tried to avoid paying me, but it wasn't the last. I definitely got better and bolder in demanding my paychecks during the economic upset.

"The wealthy woman pays herself first."
- From The Five Lessons A Millionaire Taught me for Women About Life and Wealth[9]

I wish I'd read the book "*The Five Lessons A Millionaire Taught Me for Women About Life and Wealth*" in my teens. It could have prepared me for the years of financial drought that were ahead. But alas, lessons come in their time and I'm grateful that I have finally learned some steps to take to become wealthy.

If you look to the media for what success is, you will find yourself living beyond your means and struggling to survive. The media very rarely shows the road people took before they became successful. All you see is lavish spending, partying, and then the infamous downfall. Sadly, this is what our young women are thinking when it comes to success.

While watching an episode of Tia & Tamera on the Style channel, Tamera was planning her wedding to the man of her dreams. She found out that it was going to rain on her outside wedding and that it would cost $20,000 for a tent.

"$20,000?" she said and then began to cry on her friend's shoulders.

My first thought was, what's the big deal? Isn't she well off? Then her friend began to console her and told her that she always budgeted as if she had no money and that it was okay to splurge on this very special day and get the tent. Wow...I thought to myself as I watched on. If more women could think this way, we would all be in a better financial situation.

There are plenty of debt consolidation companies and ways to secure financial freedom. The key is not to put on airs, to be honest and humble and to seek out the guidance you need.

DIVA RECAP:

- When you make it through certain situations you will be stronger and you will look back and laugh.
- If your boyfriend/BFF cries for you, it's pretty bad.
- Every job you have is meant to teach you something. Learn that lesson well.
- Don't be ashamed to talk money. Get comfortable. You will be negotiating money for the rest of your life.
- Save as much money as you can to prepare for your t-shirt selling season.

14.
OUTRO.

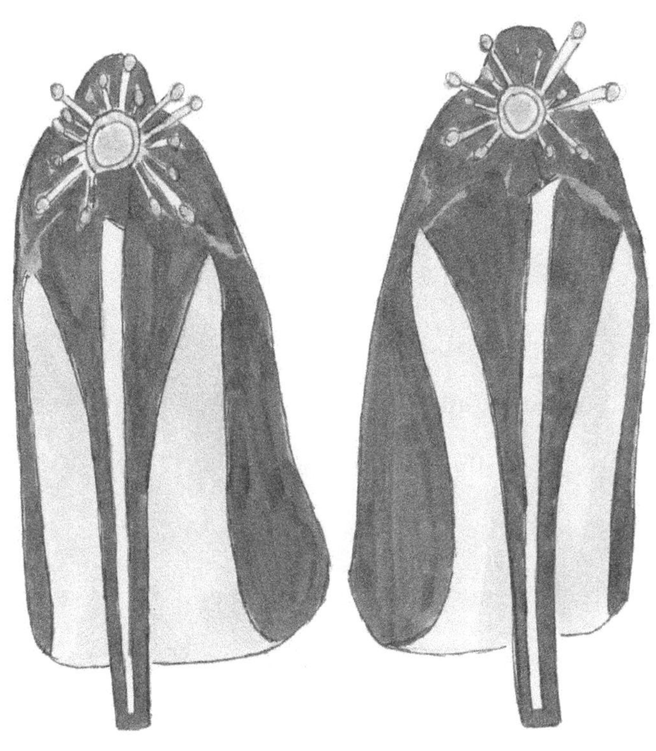

I'm a writer. But I cannot put into words how it feels to finally have completed my first book. It took almost a decade to write and get enough courage to share these lessons with the world. Admittedly, the courage took the longest for me to overcome. I wanted and still want this book to be helpful to young women. I wanted and still want the stories to be relatable. Middle school has changed and the experiences of young women today are in my opinion a bit more tough to navigate. But the lessons are still valuable and I want to share my testimony to aide you, my reader, on your journey.

As the time to publish this book came near, I was filled with doubts. Will this be helpful? Will young women understand how much they are loved and don't have to seek approval from young men or their peers? Is the message I am trying to get across clear? Will this be relatable to the teenagers now? So many questions filled my head. I started to hear the devil tell me that no one will read this and that it will not help. There was a point that I almost started to fall for that so I sent the unedited version to two people who were mentioned in the book by name: Annie and Bronwyn. Their feedback was amazing and affirming and I cast down those negative thoughts and here we are. Most of the time doubt comes right before you are supposed to do something great. Right before you are to do something that you are meant to do. It is meant to stop you from your blessing. Not this time.

I'm still not where I want to be in life. There is still so much more to learn, give, do and see. This is just part of my journey. I'm really still at the beginning. I'm seeing life in a different way as I continue to learn and grow. Everything is a lesson. Albeit sometimes hard lessons and ones that I wish I didn't have to learn in the way God decides to teach me. But I am learning to be a humble student. Well...I'm trying to be a humble student.

What I've found while writing and reliving these moments is the feeling, no matter how long ago, can bring pain, joy and laughter to me even now. The story about when I sold T-shirts outside of grocery stores was a very painful process then. But now I can laugh about it. As a matter of fact, recently I had lunch with the ex boyfriend I spoke about in that chapter and some friends and we had a HUGE laugh about it. He said he had been there and felt so sorry for me that he had to shed tears. We laughed almost to tears. That is what being on the other side of a lesson does for you.

And I keep thinking about all of the times I wanted to give up. The times I was really close to ending my life. But God. If I had given up then this book wouldn't have been finished. I wouldn't have been able to enjoy the peace that I have now. Never give up. No tough season/lesson is ever worth giving up your life. Go through but do not stay stuck in. You can do it. You are worth it.

I'm in a very blessed season in life right now. I was blessed with a promotion and then a better job all within months of each other. I started a YouTube show last year called, The Divas Circle. In each show a group of us get together and discuss different topics such as: relationships, health and lifestyle. The magazine, The Diva Inc [dot] com, has been flourishing and my creativity has been reignited. Do you realize that sometimes when you go through really tough seasons that your creativity can be suppressed? That is what happened to me. But once I went through those lessons God opened so many doors it is hard to walk through all of them at the same time. Abundance.

There are still so many stories that I want to share with you. They couldn't all fit into this book. That is why I view this, God willing, the first book in a series.

Thank You, Loves, for reading this. I pray that it blessed you in some way and that you understand how much God loves you. Your worth is not determined by your worst season or your best. Your worth is determined by God. No one can tell you that you are not loved because that goes against what God has said.

For God so loved the world that he
gave his only begotten son,
that whosoever believeth in Him shall
not perish, but have everlasting life.
John 3:16

NOTES.

1. SFGate.com, "What the most common jobs in San Francisco area pay," http://blog.sfgate.com/gettowork/2013/12/17/what-the-most-common-jobs-in-san-francisco-pay/ (accessed January 2015)
2. Bishop TD Jakes, "Transformational Creativity Sermon," https://www.youtube.com/watch?v=a6r9PFa_8Ls (accessed March 2014)
3. Carl Pickard, "Surviving (Your Child's) Adolescence," May 16, 2009, http://www.psychologytoday.com/blog/surviving-your-childs-adolescence/20095/adolescent-dating-what-makes-good-relationship (accessed January 2015)
4. Center for Disease Control and Prevention, "Suicide Prevention," http://cdc.gov/violenceprevention/pub/youth_suicide.html (accessed January 2015)
5. SuicidePreventionLifeline.org (accessed January 2015)
6. Van Moody, *The People Factor: How Building Great Relationships and Ending Bad Ones Unlocks Your God Given Purpose* (Thomas Nelson, 2014)
7. Bishop TD Jakes, "God's Got You Covered Sermon [New Year Revival 2008]," tdjakes.org
8. Nina Garcia, *The Little Black Book of Style* (HarperCollins Publishers 2007)
9. Richard Paul Evans, *The Five Lessons a Millionaire Taught Me for Women* (Touchstone 2012)

www.ingramcontent.com/pod-product-compliance
Lightning Source LLC
Chambersburg PA
CBHW030830090426
42737CB00009B/957

* 9 7 8 0 6 9 2 4 3 3 5 4 6 *